Grace Choi

A message from the author

Hello! My name is Grace Choi. I went to so many amazing places while living in Italy and got inspired to write this book. I wanted to share my experience with those who are unable to come to Italy due to COVID-19. I hope this story made you feel like going on a trip to Italy with Fluff and the stranger!

ITALY

The Way Out of
Boredom

Grace J. Choi

Austin Macauley Publishers™
LONDON • CAMBRIDGE • NEW YORK • SHARJAH

ISBN - 9789948806455 - (Paperback)
ISBN - 9789948806462 - (E-book)

Application Number: MC-10-01-0936747
Age Classification: E

Printer Name: iPrint Global Ltd
Printer Address: Witchford, England

First Published 2022
AUSTIN MACAULEY PUBLISHERS FZE
Sharjah Publishing City
P.O. Box [519201]
Sharjah, UAE
www.austinmacauley.ae
+971 655 95 202

For everyone who dreams of traveling to Italy during pandemic period.

The Very Bored
Fluff Ball

Age :   Unknown
Favorite Food :   Popcorn
Favorite Color :   Pink
Likes :   Eating Popcorn,
          Watching TV,
          Sleeping
Dislikes :   Traveling, Exercising

Prolog

It was a bright, sunny day,

but the very bored Fluff Ball just sat, nothing to say.

Bored, bored, bored,

like it was all it could afford.

Sit, sit, sit,

couldn't it just move, just one little bit?

And with a loud

BAM!

The door opened and closed with a slam.

"Hello, hello. Who are you? You don't seem to be having fun, are you?"

The stranger just waited, waiting for a sound.

She heard a little swoosh, but it was just the next-door hound.

"Well, come, come! You bored little thing! I will cure you. You'll be happier than a king! Follow me, you silent little thing. I have a great idea, the ones that go ding!"

The bored, silent Fluff finally made a sound.

"You still couldn't cure me even if you brought me with you the whole world round. If it was a world full of boredom, I'm sure I'd be crowned!"

The eager stranger gave a little nod.

"Deal! Just you wait. We'll BOTH be as happy as two peas in a pod!"

Before the Fluff Ball could moan and groan, it thought, I should have known.

"What are you waiting for? Let's go. Let's go! Get that frown off your face. we'll set off, and we'll find our way out of boredom!" And suddenly, the Fluff's fingers felt numb.

But just like that, they set off, to the way out of boredom, and the stranger said most brilliantly,

"We're going! To the exciting, far, far away Italy!"

Day 1
In Rome

"Quickly, quickly. Make yourself at home, for now, we are in the amazing, Rome!" the stranger said.

The very bored Fluff Ball looked straight ahead.

Oh, and boy, oh boy. How big its eyes grew!

And there were only a few times that happened, very few. "Standing before you is the magnificent Colosseum! Look at it carefully. You can't even see it in a museum! This is where ol' gladiators fought. People came. People were brought," the stranger explained, but the Fluff was nowhere in sight.

All she could spot was the sun that was bright.

But with a blink of an eye, the Fluff Ball was back.

It banged its armor with a loud SMACK.

"RAAAAAAAAAAAAAAAAAAAAAAAAAAAAAAAAAAAAAAAAR!" it shouted.

The Fluff Ball pictured the building as overcrowded. They looked at each other and gave a little nod. The two left as happy as two peas in a pod.

Day 2
In Naples

They walked, but then the Fluff Ball's stomach growled and it started to pout.

"I'm hungryyyyyyyyyyyyyyyyy…" it whined.

"Oh! I'm glad you said! I have an idea, up in my head!" the stranger said. "We're going to Naples, and there's something you need to know. They have a great pizza. They even make the dough!"

And just like that, they rode to the pizza paradise, Naples. Their pizza's better than the one in fables.

They headed to Ristorante Pizza, where they start fresh from dough.

The shimmer from the fresh tomatoes made them glow. "Bongiorno, what would you eat today? Here is the menu!" an Italian chef with a curled-up mustache said.

"Have the margherita!" the stranger said as she nodded. "Deep history it is. A pizza maker had to serve Queen Margherita food to show his respect. He used ingredients for the margherita: cheese, tomato sauce, and basil (which are colors of Italy). Anyway, the queen LOVED it, to conclude."

"A pizza named after Queen Margherita? I'll take that, the margherita, whatever it is!" the Fluff Ball shouted. The Fluff Ball thought it couldn't be that good. It pretty much doubted.

A few minutes later, the eager Fluff shoved a Naples pizza slice into its straight mouth.

Its eyes grew, and its highlights flickered in every direction—north, east, west, and south.

The cheese was gooey, the tomato sauce was warm, the bread was soft, and the crust was crunchy.

Anyhow, it was *really* munchy.

And good.

The happy Fluff left the place in a happy mood.

Day 3
In Florence

"Ahhh! We're going. Yes we are, where the dome is higher than a bright, shining star!"

The Fluff just stared, not knowing a thing. It definitely did NOT look happier than a king.

"Come on, don't you know? The dome of Florence! Don't just stay low! The dome, oh the dome! Come, I hope you had some practice exercise at home!"

What that meant, well, the Fluff just couldn't guess! But if it had something to do with exercise. It knew it wouldn't be a success. Knowing less and less, it just had to confess.

"NOPE," it said, but the stranger kept going. She just tilted her head.

"No. Nope. No exercise. But I AM BAD at walking," it cried. The stranger just laughed and opened her mouth, "But you've never really tried!"

So, the Fluff sat and thought.

But it was true. So it guessed it wouldn't mind getting taught. A few long hours later, they arrived.

The Fluff didn't believe the people who had visited and survived. The dome was high, TOO high for the Fluff. At least that's what it thought. It believed it had enough.

But the stranger just dragged the Fluff, and she was indeed pretty tough.

They started to climb the dome, stair after stair. The Fluff really thought it wasn't really fair.

"Saaaaaaave meeeeeeeeeee..." the Fluff whined after five minutes. But the stranger just talked about traveling having no limits.

After another set of five minutes, they had climbed one-fourth of the dome of Florence.

During the process, the Fluff made a loud and teary performance.

But stair after stair, they reached the top, and the Fluff could see it was completely fair.

The view was more beautiful than anything it had ever seen. It was incredible. It thought it only existed on a computer screen. The Fluff was amazed, but it started feeling dazed.

So later, when nearly no one was around, the stranger had to carry the Fluff down.

The Fluff was smiling as it opened its eyes again. It wondered where they would go and when.

It surely hoped soon, right after the moon!

Day 4
In Pisa

The Fluff sat happily in the car. Their destination didn't seem very far.

It smiled a big, dazed smile, it didn't complain for a while.

Well, it wasn't really a complaint, it just asked and begged for an answer, later pretended to faint.

The Fluff asked and asked, to get the answer was already tasked. "Where, where, where? What, what, what? Please tell me, or my mouth won't shut! I need to know!"

"So?" the stranger said as she glued a sly smile on her face. The Fluff was now having second thoughts about this place.

"Ah hah! At last! Watch… The Leaning Tower of Pisa!!!"

The Fluff's little, tiny eyes got big and wide. They moved quickly, side to side.

Its straight mouth started wiggling up, its eyes got hopeful, just like a pup.

And without a second thought, it ran and the tower was caught. I mean, that's what it believed. Who knows, would the 'heroic' action get people relieved?

But the people just threw it some dirty ol' looks, but the tower couldn't be leaning, those were only in books!

Or was it? The stranger moved the Fluff away, and it had to admit. It was leaning! Actually leaning! But seriously, what was the whole thing's meaning?

But the stranger shook her head, like its mind was just read. "Questions can wait, c'mon! We can't be late!"

The Fluff was dragged, it knew something was up and it frowned as it gagged.

When the Fluff was dragged, something was always up, but you couldn't escape it, so all you could basically do was sit, be sad, and gag.

Moments later, they were far away from the leaning tower. It felt a little relieved as it now regained some power.

The stranger held up a camera and told the Fluff to point its finger up.

She gave directions, until she made a loud and straight "HUP!" The Fluff froze, as the stranger whispered, "Here goes!"

And SNAP! She fanned the picture and set it on her lap. The Fluff nodded its head in approval. Maybe it wouldn't try to get people to help with the tower's removal.

The picture showed the Fluff and the Tower of Pisa, and it looked as though the Fluff were touching the highest point. But there was just one thing that was a disappointment. The Fluff's face! If only that could replace...

And as though its mind was read, again, the stranger said, "Go on, on the count of ten!"

CLICK! A photo came out. It couldn't be better, they both were sure without a doubt.

As they left, people came. They were lucky to come early. Or the photo time would've just been lame.

As they passed, the Fluff gave the Leaning Tower of Pisa a big hug and bought a souvenir mug.

"Go on, go on! We can't just spawn! Go, go! Next destination! We should've started a while ago!"

The Fluff said happily, and the stranger shook her head rapidly.

"Oh, really? Now, don't be silly. There's another day waiting for us, and we've got to be prepared."

And the Fluff just stared.

"Nighty, night! Have a good night's sleep. Just don't wake up and weep!" They both laughed as they drift and draft off to sleep.

Day 5
In Milan

The very next day, the stranger found a bunch of fluffy hot-pink hairballs. She woke up with a "HUP!" and called the Fluff to go and clean up.

The Fluff was frowning as it walked toward the hairy hairballs. "Hmph. Even shopping would be better than this. You know, those malls…　"

"Oh, you think? Then I'll spare you your sweepin' all pink." The stranger quickly clicked some buttons on an odd-looking GPS, and it showed where to go after the last fast press.

"Drivin' out of boredom! Drivin' of boredom!" she sang in a sing-song voice. The Fluff started wondering if this was a good choice.

But suddenly, the stranger disappeared and came back with shopping bags which the Fluff found unnecessarily weird.

"Dome, d-dome! Dome, d-dome! Dome, d-dome! Dome, d-dome!" she sang in a sing-song voice, all over again. But the Fluff thought about what the stranger just sang.

DOME? The Fluff tried to escape and looked for something to hang. But the Fluff was dragged, and it had no choice but to stay still. And it moaned, "I'm getting sick. I need a pill."

"Oh, THIS dome is VERY different from the one in Florence. Oh! I guess it's 'bout time I tell you! We are in… SHOPAHOLIC MILAN!!!"

"Huh. Sounds like a place where you cook eggs on a pan." The Fluff whispered to itself.

"Oh YES!" the stranger flung the car door which made the Fluff awaken, but the Fluff was just thinking about eggs and some bacon.

But as soon as the Fluff rolled outside, it was amazed! That it couldn't hide.

It couldn't find a rounded dome-top but instead saw a HUGE shop.

The Fluff disappeared and came back with shopping bags which the stranger found unnecessarily weird.

It had some shiny sunglasses and an ink-black hat. It rolled down to the stranger and awkwardly sat.

"Ummmm… Well, I guess you've figured it out! Milan equals shopping with not a single doubt!" The stranger happily smiled at the creature, like some brilliant kid, just taught by a teacher.

At first the Fluff struck some poses to go along with all the shopping, but suddenly, the Fluff's joy came to a stopping. In fact, it slowly started hopping.

Hopping AWAY from the dome, that is. Its mood changed so quickly like soda that lost its fizz.

The Fluff suddenly felt sick. Did it have to go into the dome? It hoped it wasn't quick.

But the Fluff was dragged. Dragged and dragged. That Fluff's shoulders? Boy, they sagged.

But was this really BAD for it? To find the answer would it have to wait a bit?

When they went inside the dome, they were greeted by fancy paintings. Oh, they were fancy. To know that, they didn't need any ratings.

The Fluff's straight mouth started to bend, until one tip stood still, just the other end. But then, it stopped! And the Fluff was smiling! It looked different from the Fluff with all the styling.

The stranger laughed and said, "Oh, we have a lot more places to go, but have you changed from five days ago?"

The Fluff eagerly bobbed its head, up and down. The stranger smiled and turned around.

"So many places to go… C'mon! You'll have to stay unbored though!" The stranger hopped into the car, they were going somewhere, before they spotted a star!

The Fluff was full of happiness and glee, with the stranger, you have to be non-lazy to be free!

The Fluff smiled and smiled, it looked back at its memories, so many happy ones piled and piled.

op
ng

Day 6
In Venice

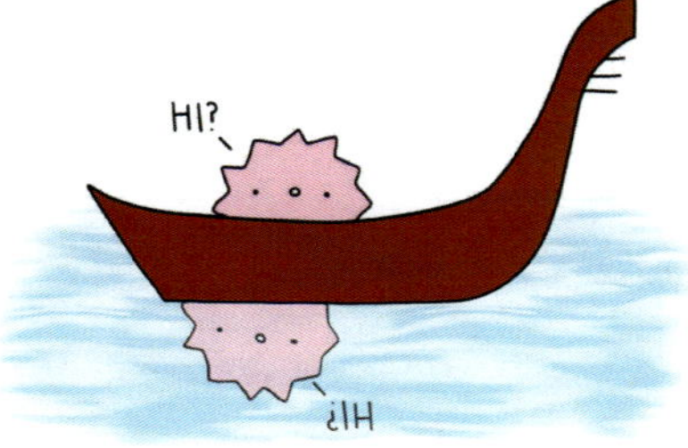

When the Fluff woke up, it almost had a heart attack. Everything seemed to go pitch black.

They were FLOATING! How was it possible? Was it really true that nothing was impossible?

The stranger laughed. "In case you are wondering, we aren't flying." The Fluff stood up, sighing.

"Then how do you explain this?" The Fluff looked down and saw another Fluff! The Fluff acted tough. So did the other one. The Fluff sat down, irritated. The stranger crossed her arms, frustrated. "Wow, you must've not even stepped outside, once! You've never been on water?" The Fluff looked at the stranger, embarrassed. "Well, this is a water city. I find those some of the rarest."

The fluffy creature stared in awe. This water city seemed to have not a single flaw.

"We are in Venice! And get ready! We are now going to pass Ponte Rialto di Venezia, the Rialto Bridge of Venice!"

The Fluff smiled as they passed beneath the beautiful bridge. It dipped its hand in the water, but it felt colder than a fridge!

After some time, they walked over the Rialto Bridge and the Fluff pleaded to go on the boat again.

"The gondola you mean?" the stranger said, pointing to the slim boat they rode before. Riding the gondola once more was all the Fluff could ask for.

So the stranger and Fluff both happily spent their time on their boat, every time feeling to float.

In Sicily

As soon as the Fluff opened its eyes, it was greeted with quite a surprise!

In front of it was a map, but it was no ordinary map. It was HUGE! But the stranger gave a snap.

"SICILY LESSON IN PROGRESS..." she half-shouted and laughed. "Come, this map is not a draft!"

Before the Fluff could speak a word, the stranger was determined to be heard. She took a deep breath and said, "Olives, wine, gelato, cheese, tomatoes, coffee, pasta, Mount Etna, hot, cold!"

She assumed the Fluff understood what she had just told. The stranger shook her head, disappointed. She looked at the map and pointed.

"In Sicily," she started slowly. "You HAVE to try ravioli! The pasta is FANTASTIC! You can also find EXTRAORDINARY olives and wine. You should see the long bar line! Oh, the gelato and coffee! Trust me, they're better than that toffee." The stranger pointed to a bowl full of coffee flavored toffee. "Sicily is warm and hot but wait 'til you get to Etna the freezing ol' mountain. I bet it's colder than a cold marble fountain!"

The stranger shivered at the thought, but she quickly changed her mood. "But the food! The food!" the stranger exclaimed. "The wondrous food! To the food, oh no. You cannot be rude!" She twirled and twirled.

"But the sun… I feel like hot ham in a bun!" the Fluff moaned and groaned. "Ah-ha! Here you go, you fluffy ol' thing! I feel like you always know what I bring! Sicily gelato, one of the best. C'mon!

Ready for a taste test?" The stranger handed a strawberry and mango gelato on a cone, and with one lick, the Fluff's mind was blown.

The chewiness, the sweetness, oh, the fruity-ness! The Fluff twirled and twirled with the stranger having fun, licking their gelato until there was none.

gelato

Day 8
In Positano

The Fluff yawned as it woke up, and the stranger filled water in a cup.

"Yup!" she said. "Vacation time, it is! Vacation is AMAZING, whether it's hers or his." She pulled on a hat and sat.

The Fluff rubbed its eyes. The stranger pulled out a hat and it gasped at its size.

It was big! VERY big! A little... Too big. But the stranger shoved the BIG hat on the Fluff and did a little jig.

"To the beach we go, where we can see the waves flow!" The stranger exclaimed and started to drive. The Fluff's jaw dropped as it arrived.

The beach was AMAZING! There was a parasol set up. Also a drink in a cup.

"Positano here we are! Enjoy, we've traveled far! Those waves, just look at how it behaves! Dark, though bright blue, a wonderful view! Those wondrous houses, someone could've worn blouses!" The Fluff looked around and saw the bright, beautiful houses.

They were so colorful they looked like bright pouches!

The Fluff pulled on its shades and went into the water, the stranger watching its wades.

Then the stranger dived in and did an impressive spin.

The two swam and splashed, and came up for their food that was secretly stashed.

They spent their time in the water and out, and this was the BEST vacation ever, without a doubt!

Day 9
In Pompeii

When the Fluff woke up, it saw that it had spilled a cup. Its fluffy fluff coat was wet, but it didn't want the Italy tour to not end yet. It stood up straight and exclaimed, "We cannot be late! Where are we going? I'm better off knowing!"

The stranger rubbed her eyes. "Can you wait until the sun starts to rise?" she whispered in a sleepy voice.

"NO!" the Fluff said.

"Then, I have no choice." The stranger stood up and hopped into the car. The sun wasn't up, but there wasn't a star.

The stranger kind of looked tired, but she was smiling.

"Oh, the happy memories piling." She smiled and stated, "We're going to Pompeii—"

"POMPEII? NOPE! I'M NOT GOING! I'VE SEEN THE VOLCANO ON TV!" The Fluff cut the stranger's words.

"Oh, Mount Vesuvius? Yes, it isn't inactive, but it hasn't erupted for YEARS. Don't worry, it's a bigger chance we have fun than we blow up," she explained. "Actually, we're going to hike to the summit of Mount Vesuvius! People say they see smoke coming out! Isn't that exciting?" the stranger happi y squealed.

"Wait what? YOU'RE going, I'm not!" The Fluff put its short little hands on its hips. It looked nervous and bit its non-existent lips.

"Well, I'm making you!" The stranger dragged the Fluff again. And the Fluff's shoulders sagged again. And the Fluff gagged again. The stranger dragged the Fluff into a car, and the driver drove. As soon as they went outside, they were greeted with a surprise!

They were IN A cloud! "WOAAAHHHHHHHHHHHHHHHHHHHHHHHH!!!!!!!!!!" the Fluff shouted unnecessarily loud.

But as much as it was cool, it was cold. "Come!" the stranger said. The Fluff felt controlled.

They walked and walked. It felt FOREVER, but after 20 – 30 minutes, they reached the summit! The Fluff's jaw dropped and almost hit the floor. There was smoke! Smoke was coming out, more and more!

The Fluff and stranger took pictures all around, and the Fluff picked up a red lava rock it found on the ground. "Wooooooooooooooooooooooowwwwww…" the Fluff whisper-shouted, remembering the smoke.

The stranger was quiet for the last few minutes, but she finally spoke.

"Amazing, huh?" she whispered, looking lost in her thoughts like the Fluff. As they went down the volcano, they saw a bar.

"Up for hot chocolate? The car isn't far!" the stranger eagerly said.

"Woah, was my mind just read?" the Fluff asked and the two sipped their hot chocolates with marshmallows inside. The two sipped and blew, happily sitting side to side.

Day 10
In Siena

The stranger came up to the Fluff like she had to say some serious stuff.

"Are you still bored? This is the…last day." the stranger whispered. The Fluff looked at the stranger and sadly whimpered. The Fluff shook its head, sadly. Suddenly the stranger exclaimed loudly.

"No time to be sad! This day is to relax! To have yummy snacks! Rewind and look back at the places we went to, and look at how much you grew. Sipping coffee, and eating croissants (they're better than the ones in restaurants!). Come on, let's go! We're going to Siena, Piazza del Campo! Here we come!"

And just like that, they set off to Piazza del Campo, Siena's Square. The stranger went to a cafe and pulled out a chair. "I'm never getting bored! Not anymore!" The Fluff looked down and smiled at the floor.

"I see that the line is bending! Look at that ending!" The stranger laughed.

    The Fluff gazed into the sky, not wanting to say bye. It loved the journey, it really did.

    Piazza del Campo was beautiful. The Fluff could see the tall clock tower. The Fluff wanted to stay there for an hour.

    The colors ginger and white created a beautiful sight.

    The stranger and Fluff both sipped and ate until it was late.

"I guess it's time I take you home. Remember Rome? And the dome?" The stranger smiled. The Fluff nodded sadly. It wanted to stay so badly.

Back Home

They both hopped into the car and drove. They were in the car for... FOREVER! But the view was amazing wherever!

They went from Siena and passed Pompeii, Positano, Sicily, Venice, Milan, Pisa, Florence, and Naples, and stopped at Rome. "That's right! You're going home!" The stranger smiled and the Fluff rolled into the plane.

The Fluff tried to figure out a way out of the plane. It was driving the Fluff insane!

It felt uncomfortable to be in a vehicle, knowing it was going home. It looked back at the trip that started in Rome.

It sighed and told itself it was lucky to have spent 10 whole days in another place! Some people stay lazy and only move when there are chips to replace.

It bent the stiff, straight mouth for the whole ride. It was smiling from side to side.

They finally got off the airplane, and the stranger and Fluff walked (the Fluff rolled) to its home.

"I'll never be lazy, I'll think of Rome and the dome!" the Fluff smiled.

The stranger smiled back.

"You, just remember to stay non-bored, okay? I wish the trip was a video you could replay," the stranger sighed. "I believe in you!" the stranger smiled one last time and SWOOSH!

All that was left was a small puff of smoke. The smoke reminded Fluff of Vesuvius, where it was so cold it wanted a cloak.

It laughed and sat down. It looked around. It noted what it saw: TV, an empty chips bowl, food crumbs, a dirty sofa, and soda.

It got right up and started to WORK! The place was too dirty! Its smile turned into a smirk.

It took the TV and sold it away. It was determined to clean the place that day.

The Fluff washed the bowl and cleaned up the crumbs. It knew the stranger would have given it two thumbs.

After some time, the place was cleaned! The place looked so clean that it gleamed!

And from that day on, the Fluff was the most active and hardworking fluff ball in town!

If the stranger was here, she might have given it a crown!

Cafe
Travel
ITALY
Travel
Kit
books

Cherished Memories

These cherished memories have led to the creation of my alter ego, The Very Bored Fluff Ball.